SHADOWS
OF
DIGITAL TRAFFIC

HIDDEN REALITIES

BOOK 1

Joshua Sodaghar

Title: *Hidden Realities: Shadows of Digital Traffic*

Author: Joshua Sodaghar

Publisher: Self-published by Joshua Sodaghar

Publishing Details:

First Edition: June 2024 Revised: August 2024 Printed in USA

Rights Statement:

Table of Contents

SHADOWS
OF
DIGITAL TRAFFIC

HIDDEN REALITIES

INTRODUCTION

I n the midst of the Windows 95 revolution, the allure of technology and the boundless possibilities of computers captivated me from those early days. My fascination with computers wasn't merely academic. As a youth, I reveled in the chaotic realms of IRC and Telnet, uncovering registry edit hacks to transform Windows themes and engaging in playful digital skirmishes with friends on AOL using tools like punters, mailbombs, Sub7, and WinNuke. These early experiences, steeped in the subculture of the internet's formative years, shaped my understanding of both the potential and the perils of the digital world. I proudly consider myself the last k-r4d, a nod to the hacker ethos of those early days.

The release of the first Matrix movie, with its intricate depiction of a dystopic world sewn within digital threads, profoundly influenced my passion for technology and hacking culture. This moment marked the beginning of a journey that would define my mindset and future career path. The journey from a curious script kiddie to working for a Fortune 500 company is a testament to the influence The Matrix series had on myself and countless others. Beyond my corporate responsibilities, I've enjoyed work as a private consultant specializing in vulnerability and risk assessments. My clients benefit from a sharp analytical mind to my ability to foresee and mitigate potential threats. My work ensures that organizations can navigate the complex and often perilous digital landscape with confidence and security.

My dedication to open-source observability and security, coupled with a staunch advocacy for privacy and encryption rights, underscores my belief in a digital world that is both transparent and secure. I strive to balance the need for robust security measures with the fundamental right to privacy.

Outside of my professional endeavors, I am a musician with two decades of experience, expressing my creativity and passion through the universal language of music. I am also an avid gamer, finding both relaxation and inspiration in the immersive worlds of online games, TCG' s and Board games.

I have witnessed firsthand the transformative impact of fake internet traffic. This book, "Hidden Realities: Shadows of Digital Traffic," is my attempt to shed light on the shadow y hands behind digital interactions, drawing from my personal experiences and extensive research.

CHAPTER 1

Origins and Evolution of Bots

In the sprawling expanse of the digital frontier, the origins of bots can be traced back to the early days of computing, where their utility and potential were first glimpsed by pioneers and hackers alike. Emerging from the fertile grounds of automation and assistance, bots began their journey as humble tools designed to streamline tasks and enhance user experience in the blooming realm of the internet.

During the nascent stages of the internet in the 1980s and 1990s, bots were conceived as rudimentary scripts programmed to automate repetitive tasks. Their initial roles ranged from fetching data from remote servers to facilitating automated responses in online chatrooms.

These early bots, while simplistic in function, laid the groundwork for future advancements in artificial intelligence and machine learning.

One notable example is the emergence of IRC (Internet Relay Chat) bots, which served as virtual assistants within chat networks. These bots, often crafted by enthusiasts within the hacker community, provided utilities such as fetching news updates, moderating discussions, or even playing text-based games. Their presence marked the intersection of creativity and functionality, showcasing the hacker ethos of repurposing technology for novel and practical ends. This also defines the Greyhat mindset of all information being open-source.

Hackers and Innovators: Pioneering Botnet Technology

As computing capabilities expanded and network infrastructures evolved, so too did the sophistication of bots. The transition from benign utilities to potent tools of exploitation begins to take shape within the underground hacker community. Motivated by curiosity, challenge, and sometimes malice, hackers explored the potential of bots to exert control over interconnected systems and devices.

The concept of botnets emerged as a pivotal innovation in the late 1990s, epitomizing the merger of automation with malicious intent. A botnet comprises a network of compromised computers, often referred to as "zombies", under the command of a central controller. This architecture allows malicious actors to orchestrate coordinated attacks, such as Distributed Denial-of-Service (DDoS) assaults or mass data exfiltration, leveraging the combined computing power of unwitting hosts.

In the veiled realm of botnets, the Botmaster reigns supreme, orchestrating chaos with precision and anonymity. This puppet master controls a network of 'zombie' computers, each infected and converted into an unwitting accomplice, executing nefarious tasks without the owner's knowledge. Central to this operation is the Command and Control (C2) server, the nerve center from which the Botmaster issues commands, directing the zombie army to launch spam and phishing campaigns, steal sensitive data, and unleash devastating DDoS attacks that can cripple entire websites. Additionally, these zombie computers generate fake internet traffic to manipulate pay-per-click advertising and inflate streaming numbers, distorting metrics and deceiving businesses and consumers alike.

The notorious Cult of the Dead Cow (cDc), a prominent hacker collective, made significant strides in botnet technology with their creation of Back Orifice in 1998. Back Orifice, a remote administration tool (RAT), enabled unauthorized access and control over remote computers, demonstrating the potential of bots as instruments of espionage and intrusion. This pioneering effort laid the groundwork for subsequent generations of botnet development and exploitation.

Simultaneously, the evolution of social media platforms introduced a new frontier for bot deployment, social bots. Unlike their predecessors focused on technical exploits, social bots infiltrated digital ecosystems to manipulate public opinion, amplify narratives, and influence collective behavior. Operated by state actors, political organizations, or commercial entities, these bots exploit algorithmic vulnerabilities to disseminate propaganda or sway electoral outcomes.

The 2016 U.S. presidential election provided a stark illustration of social bots' impact on political discourse. Automated accounts masquerading as genuine users flooded social media platforms with divisive content, amplifying polarization and disinformation.

Amidst these technological leaps and ethical dilemmas, the trajectory of bots continues to evolve. Advances in artificial intelligence, natural language processing, and machine learning empower bots with unprecedented capabilities to mimic human behavior and decision- making. These advancements, while promising efficiencies in fields ranging from customer service to healthcare diagnostics, also raise profound concerns about privacy, security, and algorithmic transparency.

Looking forward, the convergence of bots with emerging technologies such as blockchain, IoT (Internet of Things), and deepfakes heralds new frontiers in cybersecurity and digital deception. The proliferation of ransomware attacks facilitated by automated bots underscores the urgent need for robust defenses and proactive security measures in safeguarding digital infrastructures.

As we gaze deeper into the labyrinthine world of bots, from their practical origins to their pivotal roles in modern cybersecurity, we confront a landscape fraught with promise and peril. The journey through bot evolution illuminates not only technological prowess but also the ethical imperatives and societal impacts shaping their deployment.

In the chapters to come, we will unravel the intricate interplay between bots and digital traffic, exploring their influence on metrics like music streams, social media engagements, and cybersecurity risks. Through this exploration, we aim to dissect the hidden realities of digital traffic, empowering readers to navigate the complexities of an increasingly automated and interconnected world.

CHAPTER 2

Bot-Driven Distortion: Internet Traffic and Metrics Manipulation

In the underbelly of the digital world, bots lurk as silent sentinels of deception, orchestrating a complex web of manipulation across internet traffic and metrics. This chapter peers into their insidious influence, weaving together technical insights and real-world examples to illuminate the pervasive threat posed by automated adversaries.

Within the intricate ecosystem of digital commerce and content monetization, bots wield their influence with devastating effect. Consider the case of music streaming platforms where bots are deployed to artificially inflate play counts and manipulate popularity rankings. In 2021, the music industry was rocked by revelations of bot- driven fraud on platforms like Spotify, where fraudulent streams distorted royalty payouts and misrepresented artist popularity. These bots, meticulously programmed to simulate human interaction, not only defraud artists and undermine trust but also exploit algorithmic vulnerabilities to perpetuate their deceit.

Digital advertising, a cornerstone of online revenue generation, stands as a prime target for bot-driven exploitation. Click fraud,a malevolent tactic wherein bots generate fraudulent clicks on online ads,plagues advertisers with staggering financial losses. In recent years, industry reports have exposed sophisticated bot networks siphoning billions from digital ad budgets annually. The fallout extends beyond monetary losses to erode trust in advertising efficacy and skew performance metrics, perpetuating a cycle of economic subversion.

Search engine algorithms, designed to democratize access to information, face relentless manipulation from bots seeking to distort visibility and credibility. Notorious instances include the infiltration of search engine results pages (SERPs) by bot networks manipulating rankings through artificial traffic spikes and fraudulent backlinks. In 2019, Google disclosed uncovering a massive bot-driven campaign targeting search rankings, underscoring the vulnerabilities inherent in algorithmic integrity. Such manipulations not only compromise the reliability of search results but also jeopardize the competitive landscape for legitimate businesses striving for digital visibility.

Stealth Tactics: The Elusive Nature of Bot Detection

Detecting and mitigating bot-driven threats pose formidable challenges, exacerbated by the adaptive sophistication of modern bot technologies. Bots employ a myriad of evasion tactics, including IP spoofing, user- agent rotation, and distributed networks to evade traditional detection methods. The technical arms race unfolds within cybersecurity circles, where AI-powered anomaly detection systems and machine learning algorithms emerge as critical defenses against bot infiltrations. These technologies empower defenders to discern subtle behavioral patterns and distinguish genuine user interactions from automated subterfuge, albeit in an escalating battle against evolving adversarial tactics.

Looking ahead, the convergence of artificial intelligence with bot technologies heralds a paradigm shift in cyber threats. AI-powered bots, endowed with autonomous decision-making and adaptive learning capabilities, amplify the potency of malicious campaigns across IoT ecosystems, blockchain networks, and deep learning algorithms.

Moreover, the clandestine operations of bots within the deep web, facilitated by anonymizing technologies like Tor, foster illicit activities ranging from cyber espionage to underground marketplaces.

These covert channels serve as breeding grounds for bot-driven disruptions, underscoring the imperative for proactive defense strategies to mitigate emerging risks in an interconnected digital landscape.

As we continue to navigate the murky waters of bot-driven disruptions in internet traffic and metrics, the imperative for vigilance and innovation becomes ever more pronounced. This chapter has peeled back the layers of deception orchestrated by bots, revealing their pervasive impact on digital economies, advertising ecosystems, and cybersecurity landscapes. By embracing advanced detection technologies and fostering collaborative defenses, stakeholders can fortify their resilience against the evolving threats posed by AI-driven bots in the digital age.

In the forthcoming chapters, we will delve deeper into the clandestine infiltration of bots in social media platforms, influencing dating apps, finance and their utilization by nation-state actors in geopolitical maneuvers.

CHAPTER 3

The Silent Hand: ICANN & ISP 's

I n the intricate web of the internet, ICANN and ISPs hold the keys to the digital kingdom. They are the gatekeepers, the silent arbiters of online existence. Yet within their vast networks and protocols, there lies a cryptic underworld where bots roam free, manipulating metrics, influencing traffic, and altering the very fabric of our digital reality. This chapter will go into the mechanisms by which these entities inadvertently, or perhaps deliberately, facilitate bot traffic and the far- reaching consequences of their actions.

The ICANN Nexus: Gatekeeping in a Digital Age

ICANN, the Internet Corporation for Assigned Names and Numbers, stands at the epicenter of internet governance.

Responsible for the global coordination of the DNS and IP address allocation, ICANN's policies and protocols, while designed to ensure stability and security, also provide fertile ground for exploitation. The allocation of IP addresses, for instance, is a process fraught with loopholes. Bot operators exploit these loopholes to acquire vast ranges of IP addresses, creating a digital smokescreen that conceals their activities. This practice, known as IP cycling, allows bots to evade detection by constantly changing their IP addresses, rendering traditional blacklisting methods ineffective.

Internet Service Providers (ISPs) are the conduits through which all internet traffic flows. They possess the infrastructure and the capability to monitor, regulate, and potentially block bot traffic. However, the reality is far more complex. ISPs often turn a blind eye to bot activities for several reasons: economic incentives, legal ambiguities, and technical challenges.

Economically, ISPs benefit from high traffic volumes. More data flowing through their networks translates to higher revenue, especially in markets where bandwidth usage is monetized. Bots, with their incessant requests and data consumption, inadvertently boost traffic figures, providing a financial disincentive for ISPs to take stringent action against them.

Legally, the landscape is murky. While laws against cybercrime exist, the enforcement is often lax and the definitions are ambiguous. ISPs operating in this gray area find it easier to maintain the status quo than to engage in proactive bot mitigation efforts. Moreover, the technical complexity of distinguishing legitimate traffic from bot traffic without infringing on user privacy rights presents a significant hurdle.

Case Study: The Mirai Botnet

To illustrate the complicity and the consequences, consider the infamous Mirai botnet. In 2016, Mirai orchestrated one of the most devastating DDoS attacks in history, targeting Dyn, a major DNS provider. The attack disrupted major websites like Twitter, Netflix, and Reddit, highlighting the vulnerabilities in our digital infrastructure.

Mirai's success hinged on its ability to exploit IoT devices, which were poorly secured and ubiquitously connected. These devices, scattered across the globe and linked by ISPs, formed an army of bots capable of overwhelming even the most robust defenses. The role of ISPs in this scenario was crucial,they were the unwitting enablers, providing the connectivity and the bandwidth that fueled Mirai's assault.

The DNS, overseen by ICANN, is the internet's phonebook, translating human-friendly domain names into IP addresses. This system, while essential for web navigation, is also a prime target for exploitation by bots. DNS amplification attacks, a common tactic employed by botnets, involve sending a small query to a DNS server, which then responds with a much larger payload to the target, amplifying the impact of the attack.

Moreover, DNS manipulation by bots can lead to traffic redirection, where users attempting to visit a legitimate site are instead funneled to malicious pages. This not only compromises user security but also skews web traffic metrics, undermining the integrity of digital analytics and advertising revenues.

The economic implications of bot traffic are profound. Digital advertising, a multi-billion dollar industry, is particularly vulnerable.

Bots generate fraudulent clicks and impressions, siphoning off advertising budgets and distorting performance metrics. This not only results in financial losses but also undermines the credibility of digital advertising as a whole.

Market manipulation is another facet of bot-induced economic distortion. Bots can create artificial trading volumes in financial markets, influencing stock prices and cryptocurrency valuations.

Combating bot traffic requires a multi-faceted approach, integrating advanced technologies and collaborative efforts. Machine learning algorithms are being deployed to analyze traffic patterns and identify anomalies indicative of bot activity. These systems, constantly evolving, offer a proactive defense mechanism against the ever-adaptive nature of bots.

ISPs too have a critical role to play. Implementing stricter monitoring protocols and leveraging AI-driven analytics can help identify and mitigate bot traffic at the network level. However, this requires a shift in priorities, balancing economic incentives with the imperative for cybersecurity.

As we methodically unravel the intricate layers of digital traffic, the unsettling truth about the role of ICANN and ISPs in abetting bot activity and perpetuating fake internet traffic comes starkly into focus.

Positioned as gatekeepers to the internet, these entities wield immense power coupled with an equally significant responsibility.

In this bold and uncertain digital frontier, vigilance and innovation emerge as our paramount allies. As we venture deeper into the obscured realms of our interconnected world, it is through the harmonious fusion of open-source methodologies and progressive technological advances that we will forge a future. In this future, the murky shadows cast by digital traffic do not loom as ominous threats but stand as challenges addressed with relentless determination and creative ingenuity.

The ensuing chapters will explore further into these shadows, exploring them through case studies and technical analysis.

Here we will uncover not just the mechanisms of exploitation and control but also the strategies and tools at our disposal to dismantle and rebuild a more secure, transparent digital world.

CHAPTER 4

Digital Deception:
The Bot Infiltration

The digital landscape is rife with deception. Social media platforms, dating apps, and online forums, once heralded as the bastions of open communication and human connection, have become the playgrounds for bots. These digital entities, masquerading as real users, manipulate metrics, sway public opinion, and disrupt the very fabric of online interaction. This chapter goes into the technical intricacies and use cases of bot infiltration, exposing the depth of their influence and the challenges in combating them.

Social bots are designed to mimic human behavior on social media platforms. They create fake profiles, post updates, like, share, and comment, all while following pre-programmed instructions. These bots are more than mere nuisances; they are tools for mass manipulation and disinformation.

Technical Analysis:

Botnets and Coordination: These social bots operated in a coordinated manner, forming botnets that could trend hashtags, manipulate algorithms, and create viral content. By analyzing traffic patterns, researchers identified synchronized posting behaviors and IP cycling techniques, revealing the vast network of automated accounts.

Natural Language Processing (NLP): Advanced bots employed NLP to generate human-like text, making their posts and interactions difficult to distinguish from those of real users. Sentiment analysis algorithms were utilized to tailor content to elicit emotional responses, further enhancing their persuasive power.

Dating apps, designed to foster connections, have also fallen prey to bot infiltration. Bots on these platforms engage with users, lure them into conversations, and often direct them to fraudulent sites or scams. The emotional and financial toll of these interactions can be devastating.

Case Study: The Ashley Madison Hack

In 2015, the infidelity dating site Ashley Madison was hacked, revealing that a significant portion of female profiles were actually bots created to engage male users. This deception not only damaged the site's credibility but also highlighted the widespread use of bots to inflate user engagement metrics. Future chapters will elaborate more on this infamous hack.

Technical Analysis:

Automated Interaction Scripts: Bots on dating apps use predefined scripts to initiate and sustain conversations. These scripts are often sophisticated, incorporating NLP to adapt responses based on user input. The use of machine learning allows these bots to improve their conversational abilities over time, making them increasingly convincing.

Data Mining and Profiling: Bots gather personal information from users, which can be used for targeted advertising, identity theft, or further social engineering attacks. By analyzing chat logs and interaction patterns, it's possible to identify the data points bots are most interested in and how they exploit this information.

Online forums and comment sections, meant to be platforms for open discourse, are often overrun by bots. These bots can steer conversations, drown out dissenting voices, and create a false consensus, significantly impacting public perception and discourse.

In 2017, Reddit banned several accounts linked to a botnet that was manipulating discussions on political subreddits.

These bots upvoted certain posts, downvoted others, and spammed comments to shift the narrative in favor of specific political agendas.

Technical Analysis:

Vote Manipulation: Bots can artificially inflate or deflate the visibility of posts and comments through coordinated upvoting and downvoting. This skews the perceived popularity and credibility of content, affecting user engagement and platform algorithms.

IP Obfuscation: To avoid detection, bots use techniques such as IP obfuscation and VPNs. By rotating IP addresses and using proxy servers, they mask their origin, making it challenging for moderators and automated systems to identify and ban them.

Nation-state actors leverage bots for information warfare, using them to conduct espionage, disseminate propaganda, and disrupt political processes. These operations are highly sophisticated, often involving state-of-the-art technology and substantial resources.

Case Study: Operation Ghostwriter

Operation Ghostwriter, attributed to a group linked to the Belarusian government, involved the use of bots to spread disinformation and influence public opinion across Europe.

These bots hacked into legitimate news sites to post fake articles and amplified these articles through social media bots.

Technical Analysis:

Cross-Platform Synchronization: Bots used in information warfare often operate across multiple platforms simultaneously. They can launch coordinated attacks, ensuring that disinformation spreads rapidly and broadly. This synchronization is achieved through advanced botnet management tools that allow operators to control thousands of bots in real time.

AI-Driven Content Generation: To maintain credibility and evade detection, these bots use AI-driven content generation tools. These tools can create fake news articles, social media posts, and comments that closely mimic human language and behavior. By integrating AI with big data analytics, operators can tailor their disinformation campaigns to specific demographics and regions.

While the infiltration of bots into social media and online platforms is a growing concern, there are ongoing efforts to combat this threat. However, the dynamic and adaptive nature of bots presents significant challenges.

One of the most promising approaches to detecting and mitigating bot activity is through machine learning and behavioral analysis. By training algorithms to recognize patterns indicative of bot behavior, platforms can identify and block bots more effectively.

Pattern Recognition: Machine learning models can analyze large datasets to identify patterns in posting frequency, content similarity, and interaction behavior. These patterns help distinguish bots from legitimate users, even when bots use advanced evasion techniques.

Behavioral Biometrics: Analyzing the way users interact with their devices, such as typing speed, mouse movements, and touch patterns, can provide additional indicators of bot activity. Bots often exhibit mechanical and consistent interaction patterns that differ from human behavior.

Legal and regulatory measures are also being explored to address the proliferation of bots. However, the global and decentralized nature of the internet makes enforcement a complex issue. We should also keep in mind that government and regulations should never be an option for the internet. You know what they say, put the government in charge of the Sahara Desert and it will run out of sand within a year.

Transparency Requirements: Proposed regulations may require platforms to disclose automated accounts and provide users with tools to report suspected bots. Increased transparency can help users recognize and avoid bot interactions. Private companies, ISPs, and ICANN should take a more proactive approach to bot detection and fake internet traffic that they have allowed to become out of control for nearly 30 years.

In the ever-expanding arsenal of digital deception, drive-by pharming stands out as a particularly stealthy and dangerous tactic. This method exploits vulnerabilities in routers, redirecting users' DNS settings without their awareness and leading them to malicious websites designed to harvest credentials, install malware, or further entrench botnet control. Drive-by pharming is especially insidious when combined with bot networks. By quietly hijacking routers and redirecting traffic on a large scale, attackers can turn unwitting victims into participants in their schemes, further fueling bot-driven operations like Pay-Per-Click (PPC) fraud. In this context, bots click on ads with the intent of generating fraudulent revenue, manipulating digital metrics, and distorting the integrity of online advertising ecosystems. This form of attack underscores the adaptability of botnets and their operators, who continually evolve their methods to exploit new vulnerabilities. As drive-by pharming becomes increasingly sophisticated, it not only compromises individual devices but also reinforces the broader infrastructure of bot infiltration, making detection and prevention even more challenging.

Case Study: The DNSChanger Malware Drive-By Pharming

In one of the most infamous instances of drive-by pharming, this malware was used to execute a massive global attack that compromised over 4 million computers across more than 100 countries between 2007 and 2011. The malware altered the DNS settings of infected routers, redirecting unsuspecting users to rogue servers controlled by the attackers. DNSChanger spread primarily through malicious advertisements on websites and phishing emails. Once a user clicked on a compromised ad or link, the malware would silently exploit vulnerabilities in their router, changing its DNS settings to point to rogue DNS servers controlled by the attackers. This drive-by pharming technique enabled the attackers to reroute all internet traffic from the infected devices to malicious sites without the users' knowledge.

Attackers used this redirected traffic for a variety of fraudulent purposes, including Pay-Per-Click (PPC) fraud, where they generated millions of dollars by directing users to websites that paid for traffic. Additionally, the rogue DNS servers could redirect users to phishing sites designed to steal personal and financial information, further exacerbating the damage. The scale of the attack was unprecedented, affecting not only individual users but also businesses, government agencies, and educational institutions. The malware also had the capability to disable security updates and antivirus programs, leaving infected systems vulnerable to further exploitation. Mitigation and Aftermath: The operation was eventually dismantled in 2011 when the FBI, in cooperation with international law enforcement agencies, took down the rogue DNS servers in an operation known as Operation Ghost Click. However, the operation also revealed the broader vulnerabilities in the internet infrastructure that drive-by pharming exploits.

DNSChanger serves as a powerful example of how botnet capabilities can be leveraged to create widespread disruption and financial gain. It underscores the importance of securing DNS settings and the routers that control them, as well as the need for continuous vigilance against evolving cyber threats.

International Cooperation: The Botnet Empire

The cross-border nature of bot operations demands a strategic rethinking of how we approach cybersecurity. The conventional push for more regulations, though well-intentioned, often results in bureaucratic red tape that stifles innovation and impedes swift action. Instead, we must pivot towards a model of international cooperation that prioritizes agility and real-time intelligence sharing.

Botnets transcend national boundaries with ease, the effectiveness of any defense hinges on seamless collaboration. Intelligence sharing between nations should be the cornerstone of our anti-bot measures, enabling a proactive stance against emerging threats. Rather than enforcing a one-size-fits-all policy, collaboration allows for flexibility and adaptability, ensuring that measures are tailored to the unique challenges faced by each jurisdiction.

Enforcement efforts must be streamlined, cutting through the layers of unnecessary regulation that often delay critical responses. By fostering alliances that emphasize mutual support and resource sharing, we can enhance our collective resilience against the pervasive threat of bot operations.

This approach fortifies our defenses while also champions the spirit of innovation, allowing for the development of sophisticated, cutting-edge solutions. In a world where cyber threats evolve at an unprecedented pace, less regulation and more strategic cooperation is not just a preference, it is an imperative for securing our digital future.

The infiltration of bots into social media, dating apps, and online forums represents a significant threat to the integrity of online interactions. As bots become more sophisticated and their operators more resourceful, the challenge of combating them intensifies. By harnessing the power of technical innovation and fostering international cooperation, we can start to reclaim the digital landscape from these elusive manipulators.

In the next chapter, we will explore how bots and botnets are employed by bad nation-state actors to further their geopolitical agendas. By understanding these advanced threats, we can better prepare for the evolving landscape of cyber warfare and digital deception.

CHAPTER 5

Nation-State Actors and the Weaponization of Bots

In the clandestine world of cyber warfare, nation-state actors have harnessed the power of bots and botnets as formidable weapons. These entities deploy bots not just for espionage but to manipulate public opinion, disrupt political processes, and destabilize economies. This chapter will give insight into the dark unknown realm of nation- state bot operations, illustrating their sophisticated techniques and the profound impact they have on global security.

Nation-states have long grasped the strategic prowess of bots. These digital soldiers, masters of deception, execute operations spanning cyber espionage, psychological warfare, and devastating DDoS tactics, all cloaked in plausible deniability. In an instant, they unleash torrents of disinformation or orchestrate precision cyberattacks, disrupting and destabilizing their targets with ruthless efficiency.

Case Study: The Stuxnet Worm

Stuxnet, a sophisticated computer worm discovered in 2010, was reportedly developed by the United States and Israel to sabotage Iran's nuclear program. While not a bot in the traditional sense, Stuxnet demonstrated the potential of state-sponsored malware. Its ability to infiltrate and disrupt critical infrastructure underscored the destructive power of cyber weapons.

Technical Analysis:

Propagation Techniques: Stuxnet spread through removable drives and network shares, employing multiple zero-day vulnerabilities to infect its targets. This method of propagation is akin to how botnets spread across networks, exploiting weak points to secure a foothold.

Command and Control (C2) Infrastructure: The worm communicated with its handlers via a sophisticated C2 infrastructure. This allowed the operators to issue commands, update the malware, and exfiltrate data, a technique commonly used by botnets to maintain control over infected systems.

SHADOWS OF DIGITAL TRAFFIC

The integrity of democratic processes has increasingly come under threat from nation-state actors using bots to interfere in elections. These operations aim to sow discord, influence voter behavior, and undermine trust in electoral systems.

Case Study: Russian Interference in the 2016 US Presidential Election

The Russian government's interference in the 2016 US Presidential Election was a multifaceted operation deploying an intricate web of social media bots, trolls, and state-sponsored hackers. This covert campaign aimed to manipulate public opinion and undermine trust in the democratic process. Central to this operation was the Internet Research Agency (IRA), a notorious Russian entity. Despite spending a mere $100,000 on Facebook ads, a paltry sum for nation-state actors, the IRA effectively swayed online conversations, driving narratives both for and against various parties and candidates. This minimal investment highlights the profound impact and efficiency of digital disinformation tactics in modern geopolitical strategies.

Technical Analysis:

Social Media Manipulation: Bots were used to create and amplify divisive content, targeting specific demographic groups to exacerbate social tensions. By analyzing bot activity, researchers identified patterns of coordinated behavior, such as simultaneous posting and retweeting of propaganda.

Phishing and Hacking: State-sponsored hackers employed phishing attacks to gain access to email accounts and sensitive data. This information was then weaponized by bots, which disseminated it strategically to maximize its impact.

Bots can also be used to destabilize economies and disrupt markets. Through financial market manipulation, intellectual property theft, and attacks on supply chains, nation-state actors can inflict significant economic damage on their adversaries.

Case Study: The 2017 NotPetya Attack

The NotPetya malware, attributed to the Russian military, caused widespread disruption across Ukraine and beyond. It masqueraded as ransomware but was designed to inflict maximum damage, crippling businesses and critical infrastructure.

Technical Analysis:

Wiper Malware: Unlike traditional ransomware, NotPetya irreversibly encrypted data, effectively destroying it. This tactic is reminiscent of botnet-driven Distributed Denial of Service (DDoS) attacks, which aim to disrupt rather than extort.

Lateral Movement: NotPetya employed techniques such as credential dumping and SMB exploitation to move laterally within networks. This allowed it to spread rapidly and infect multiple systems, a strategy commonly used by botnets to expand their reach.

In the realm of psychological warfare, bots are deployed to manipulate public perception and control narratives. By flooding social media with propaganda and disinformation, nation-state actors can shape opinions and incite unrest.

Case Study: The Chinese Government's Use of Bots in Hong Kong Protests

During the Hong Kong protests in 2019, the Chinese government used bots to spread disinformation and pro-Beijing narratives. These bots aimed to discredit the protesters and create confusion among the public.

Technical Analysis:

Astroturfing: Bots created fake grassroots movements, making it appear as though large numbers of people supported pro-government stances. This technique, known as astroturfing, leverages the perceived authenticity of organic social movements to spread propaganda.

Doxxing and Intimidation: Bots were also used to doxx protesters, revealing their personal information and subjecting them to harassment. By automating these attacks, the perpetrators could target a large number of individuals simultaneously, amplifying the psychological impact.

Nation-state actors exploit a range of advanced techniques and tools to enhance the effectiveness of their bot operations. Understanding these methods is crucial for developing strategies to counteract them.

AI and machine learning are increasingly being integrated into botnets to enhance their capabilities. These technologies enable bots to adapt and improve their behavior, making them more effective and harder to detect.

Adaptive Learning: Bots can use machine learning algorithms to analyze user behavior and adapt their interactions accordingly. This makes them more convincing and capable of evading detection mechanisms that rely on static behavioral patterns.

Deepfakes and Synthetic Media: AI-driven bots can generate deepfake videos and synthetic media to create realistic but false content. These tools are used to deceive and manipulate audiences, further blurring the line between reality and fabrication.

The use of blockchain and decentralized networks provides bots with enhanced anonymity and resilience. These technologies make it more difficult to trace and disrupt botnet operations.

Decentralized Command and Control: By using blockchain-based C2 systems, botnet operators can avoid the single points of failure inherent in traditional C2 infrastructures. This decentralization makes it harder for authorities to shut down botnets.

The weaponization of bots by nation-state actors represents a significant threat to global security. These digital mercenaries are capable of executing a wide range of operations, from election interference and economic sabotage to psychological warfare and cyber espionage. As technology continues to evolve, so too will the sophistication and impact of these bot operations.

In the next chapter, we will explore deeper how these bots and botnets find their way into social media, dating apps, and online forums, perpetuating their influence and expanding their reach. By examining these platforms, we can better understand the tactics employed by bot operators and develop strategies to mitigate their impact.

CHAPTER 6

Social Media Manipulation and the Perils of Fake Profiles

In the sprawling digital landscape of social media, bots have found fertile ground to sow discord, spread misinformation, and manipulate public opinion. These platforms, originally designed to connect people, have become battlegrounds where armies of bots wage silent wars. This chapter will will show the pervasive presence of bots in social media, their sophisticated techniques, and the far-reaching consequences of their activities.

Social media platforms are prime targets for bot operations due to their vast user bases and influential nature. Bots infiltrate these platforms using a variety of methods, from creating fake profiles to hijacking existing accounts. Their primary objectives range from spreading propaganda and disinformation to manipulating engagement metrics and influencing trends.

Phantom Followers: The Dark Arts of Bot Farms

Large-scale operations known as bot farms operate with silent efficiency, managing and orchestrating thousands of fake profiles. These digital marionettes are meticulously crafted to like, share, and comment on posts, fabricating the illusion of widespread support or opposition.

The synthetic activity generated by these bot farms is not mere noise; it is a calculated attempt to shape perceived trends, influencing public opinion and manipulating online narratives. This covert manipulation raises urgent questions about the integrity of online discourse and the unseen forces steering the digital zeitgeist.

AI-Driven Content Generation: Advanced bots utilized AI to generate and disseminate content that mimicked human language and behavior. This made the disinformation campaigns more convincing and harder to detect.

Fake profiles are the bread and butter of social media bots. These profiles can be used for a variety of malicious purposes, including identity theft, social engineering, and phishing attacks. By creating convincing personas, bots can gain the trust of real users and exploit them in numerous ways.

Case Study: The Ashley Madison Hack

In 2015, the dating site Ashley Madison was hacked, exposing the personal information of millions of users. Investigations revealed that a significant portion of the site's female profiles were bots designed to engage with male users. These bots were used to keep users active on the site and generate revenue.

Technical Analysis:

Automated Engagement: Bots on dating sites like Ashley Madison used algorithms to initiate and maintain conversations with users. These interactions were designed to keep users engaged and encourage them to spend money on the platform.

Data Mining: The information gathered by these bots was often used for data mining purposes, providing valuable insights into user behavior and preferences. This data could then be sold to third parties or used for targeted marketing campaigns.

Bots on social media are also employed for psychological operations (psyops) and propaganda. By creating and amplifying specific narratives, bots can shape public perception and influence societal behavior. This is particularly dangerous in times of political unrest or during critical events.

Case Study: The Hong Kong Protests

During the 2019 Hong Kong protests, a sophisticated campaign of digital warfare emerged, with Chinese state-sponsored bots inundating social media platforms with pro-government narratives and disinformation. These bots were instrumental in efforts to delegitimize the protesters and tilt public sentiment in favor of the Chinese government's narrative.

Technical Analysis:

Astroturfing Campaigns: The deployment of bots created an illusion of widespread community-driven support for the government's position. This practice, known as astroturfing, exploits the perceived authenticity of organic social movements to disseminate propaganda, making state-sponsored messages appear as genuine public opinion.

Doxxing and Harassment: In a more aggressive tactic, bots were utilized to dox and harass protestors. By automating these malicious activities, the perpetrators were able to target a vast number of individuals simultaneously, significantly amplifying the psychological stress and intimidation faced by the protestors.

The Technical Arsenal of Social Media Bots

Bots on social media platforms employ a variety of sophisticated techniques to evade detection and maximize their effectiveness. Understanding these techniques is crucial for developing strategies to combat them.

Modern bots are equipped with AI capabilities that allow them to mimic human behavior. This makes them more difficult to detect and allows them to interact more convincingly with real users.

Natural Language Processing (NLP): Bots use NLP algorithms to generate text that appears natural and human-like. This enables them to engage in realistic conversations and avoid detection by automated systems.

Behavioral Mimicry: Bots analyze the behavior of real users and mimic their actions. This includes posting patterns, language usage, and engagement with content. By blending in with legitimate users, bots can operate undetected for longer periods.

Bots employ various evasion techniques to avoid detection by platform moderators and automated security systems. These techniques include rotating IP addresses, using proxies, and leveraging compromised accounts.

IP Rotation and Proxies: Bots frequently change their IP addresses and use proxies to mask their true location. This makes it difficult for security systems to track their activity and block their access.

Account Hijacking: Instead of creating new profiles, some bots hijack existing accounts. This allows them to bypass security measures that target newly created accounts and exploit the trust associated with established profiles.

The presence of bots on social media distorts metrics and degrades the user experience. Fake likes, shares, and comments skew engagement statistics, leading to misleading conclusions about the popularity and influence of content.

Case Study: Instagram Bot Armies

Instagram has been plagued by bot armies that inflate follower counts and engagement metrics. These bots are used by influencers and brands to create the illusion of popularity, often deceiving both users and advertisers.

Technical Analysis:

Engagement Pods: Bots are organized into engagement pods where they automatically like, comment on, and share each other's posts. This creates a feedback loop that artificially boosts engagement metrics.

Fake Follower Services: Numerous services offer fake followers for a fee. These services use bots to quickly increase the follower count of a user, making them appear more popular than they actually are.

Social media bots is a testament to the lengths to which malicious actors will go to manipulate and deceive. By understanding the tactics and techniques employed by these bots, we can begin to unmask the digital puppeteers pulling the strings. In the next chapter, we will explore the current and future threats posed by bots and botnets, delving into their impact on IoT, Blockchain, Deepfakes, and ransomware. As we continue to navigate the complexities of the digital landscape, it is essential to remain vigilant and informed, arming ourselves with the knowledge to counteract these insidious threats.

CHAPTER 7

The Nexus of Bots and Cybersecurity

The digital age has ushered in an era where connectivity is a double- edged sword. As our lives become increasingly intertwined with technology, the vulnerabilities we face grow more complex and insidious. At the heart of many modern cybersecurity threats lies the ubiquitous bot, a digital entity capable of wreaking havoc on an unprecedented scale. This chapter explores the intersection of botnets with IoT vulnerabilities, the implications of bots on blockchain security, and their role in the proliferation of deepfakes and ransomware.

The Internet of Things (IoT) represents a new frontier of interconnected devices, from smart refrigerators to industrial control systems. While IoT devices promise enhanced convenience and efficiency, they also introduce significant security risks. Many IoT devices are designed with minimal security features, making them prime targets for botnets.

Case Study: The Mirai Botnet Attack

In 2016, the Mirai botnet demonstrated the catastrophic potential of exploiting IoT vulnerabilities. This botnet harnessed the power of thousands of compromised IoT devices, such as security cameras and routers, to launch massive Distributed Denial of Service (DDoS) attacks. The most notable target was Dyn, a major DNS provider, resulting in widespread internet outages.

Technical Analysis:

Default Credentials: The Mirai botnet capitalized on IoT devices with factory-default usernames and passwords. By scanning the internet for devices with these weak credentials, Mirai could easily compromise and enlist them into its botnet.

DDoS Amplification: Once compromised, these devices were used to flood targets with traffic, overwhelming their servers and rendering them inaccessible. The scale of the attack was amplified by the sheer number of devices involved.

As IoT adoption continues to rise, so too does the threat landscape. Future botnets are likely to exploit more sophisticated vulnerabilities, such as firmware flaws and unpatched software.

Firmware Exploits: Many IoT devices run outdated firmware with known security flaws. Botnets can exploit these vulnerabilities to gain control over devices and launch coordinated attacks.

Unsecured Communication Protocols: IoT devices often use unsecured communication protocols, making them susceptible to man-in-the- middle attacks. Botnets can intercept and manipulate data transmitted between devices, leading to potential breaches of sensitive information.

Blockchain technology, often hailed as the pinnacle of secure digital transactions, is not immune to the threat posed by bots. While the decentralized nature of blockchain provides inherent security advantages, it also presents unique challenges.

Case Study: The DAO Hack

In 2016, the Decentralized Autonomous Organization (DAO), a blockchain-based venture capital fund, was compromised by a hacker who exploited a vulnerability in its smart contract. The attacker siphoned off approximately $50 million worth of Ether, highlighting the risks associated with automated blockchain operations.

Technical Analysis:

Smart Contract Vulnerabilities: The DAO hack exploited a recursive call vulnerability in the smart contract code. This allowed the attacker to repeatedly withdraw funds before the contract could update its balance.

Automated Exploitation: Bots can be programmed to identify and exploit vulnerabilities in smart contracts automatically. These bots scan the blockchain for exploitable contracts, launching attacks without human intervention.

Sybil attacks pose another significant threat to blockchain networks. In a Sybil attack, an adversary creates multiple fake identities to gain control over the network, potentially undermining its security and integrity.

Consensus Manipulation: Bots can be used to create and manage these fake identities, overwhelming the network and manipulating the consensus process. This can lead to double-spending attacks and other forms of fraud.

Resource Drain: Bots participating in Sybil attacks can also drain network resources, slowing down transaction processing and compromising the overall efficiency of the blockchain.

The advent of artificial intelligence has given rise to deepfakes and ransomware, two of the most insidious threats in the cybersecurity landscape. Bots play a crucial role in the creation and dissemination of these digital menaces.

Deepfakes: A New Era of Digital Deception

Deepfakes leverage AI to create highly realistic but entirely fabricated videos and images. These can be used to spread misinformation, blackmail individuals, or even disrupt political processes.

A chilling milestone was reached in late 2022 when a deepfake video surfaced, masterfully engineered to depict a high-ranking U.S. military official. This video, a digital specter, broadcasted a dire ultimatum to a rival nation, articulating detailed military strategies and covert operations that were allegedly poised to unfold in response to the geopolitical tensions simmering between the nations.

The fabrication was alarmingly sophisticated, employing advanced machine learning algorithms, it captured not only the precise likeness but also the voice modulation and idiosyncratic mannerisms of the official in question. The deepfake emerged at a time rife with diplomatic fragility, thereby lending a disturbing credence to its contents. It propagated rapidly across media channels, sowing confusion and fear among international observers and policymakers.

The ramifications were profound and multifaceted:

- Diplomatic Fallout: Immediate and severe, the video exacerbated existing tensions, precipitating a flurry of emergency diplomatic engagements. Nations found themselves grappling not only with the content but also with the sinister implications of such technological misuse.

- Public Unrest and Fear: The video incited public unrest, as populations braced for imminent conflict. The stock markets faltered, and global security alerts soared, reflecting the palpable fear that gripped nations on the brink.

- Security Protocols and International Law: This incident catalyzed an urgent international dialogue on digital authenticity, spearheading initiatives to bolster defenses against the manipulation of digital media. It underscored an acute need for international legal frameworks to address the burgeoning threat posed by deepfake technologies.

This case study, while a harrowing echo of what might have been, serves as a stark admonition of the disruptive potential of deepfake technology. It compels a rigorous scrutiny of the ethical boundaries of digital content creation and a reinforced commitment to developing sophisticated verification technologies. The specter of a deepfake- induced crisis illuminates the perilous intersection of technology and international security, urging a vigilant and proactive stance in the digital age.

Technical Analysis:

Generative Adversarial Networks (GANs): Deepfakes are created using GANs, a class of AI algorithms that pit two neural networks against each other. One network generates the fake content, while the other attempts to detect it. This iterative process results in highly realistic forgeries.

Bot-Driven Dissemination: Bots are instrumental in spreading deepfakes across social media platforms. By rapidly sharing and liking these videos, bots can manipulate engagement metrics and ensure the content reaches a wide audience before it can be debunked.

Ransomware has evolved from simple malware into a sophisticated criminal enterprise. Bots facilitate the spread of ransomware by automating the delivery and execution of the malicious payload.

Case Study: The WannaCry Outbreak

In 2017, the WannaCry ransomware attack infected over 200,000 computers across 150 countries. The ransomware exploited a vulnerability in Windows operating systems, encrypting users' data and demanding ransom payments in Bitcoin.

Technical Analysis:

Exploit Kits: Bots deploy exploit kits to scan for vulnerable systems and deliver ransomware payloads. These kits contain pre-packaged exploits that target known vulnerabilities in software and operating systems.

Command and Control (C2) Servers: Once a system is infected, the ransomware bot communicates with a C2 server to receive instructions and encryption keys. This decentralized approach makes it difficult for authorities to shut down the operation.

Ransomware-as-a-Service (RaaS) has democratized cyber extortion, allowing even low-skilled criminals to launch sophisticated attacks. RaaS platforms provide would-be attackers with all the tools they need to distribute ransomware and collect payments.

Affiliate Programs: RaaS platforms operate affiliate programs where attackers earn a commission for each successful ransom payment. Bots play a critical role in distributing the ransomware and managing the payment infrastructure.

Automated Targeting: RaaS bots automatically target vulnerable systems, often focusing on specific industries or regions to maximize the likelihood of payment.

The nexus of bots and cybersecurity threats is a complex and ever- evolving landscape. As bots become more sophisticated, their ability to exploit vulnerabilities and orchestrate attacks will only increase.

Understanding the technical intricacies and real-world implications of these threats is essential for developing robust defenses and mitigating their impact.

In the next chapter, we will explore the current and future threats posed by bots and botnets on IoT, Blockchain, Deepfakes, and ransomware. As we continue to navigate the complexities of the digital landscape, it is essential to remain vigilant and informed, arming ourselves with the knowledge to counteract these insidious threats.

CHAPTER 8

The Ghost Code: Darknet Bots

F ar beyond the reach of conventional search engines, lies the darknet, a cryptic realm where anonymity reigns and illicit activities flourish. This digital netherworld, accessible only through specialized networks like Tor, serves as a sanctuary for those who seek to operate under the radar of conventional oversight. Yet, beyond even the well-trodden paths of Tor, lesser-known conduits offer sanctuary to a myriad of automated entities, bots that operate in shadow, conducting their clandestine activities with chilling precision. This chapter goes deep into the obscured realms where these digital specters thrive, their mechanisms, operations, and the obscure networks they inhabit.

Technical Analysis:

Crawlers: These relentless data miners index hidden websites, scraping sensitive information from the darkest corners of the deep web. Crawlers surface as frequent visitors in hidden forums and marketplaces, gathering and storing data for various purposes.

Trading Bots: Automate illicit transactions, from drug deals to weapons sales, in darknet marketplaces. Their precision and speed make them indispensable to cybercriminals. Trading bots often appear during peak trading hours, executing rapid transactions that human operators cannot match.

Malicious Bots: Deploy devastating cyberattacks, spread sophisticated malware, and conduct relentless denial-of-service assaults. These bots are typically launched from compromised devices within decentralized networks, making their detection and neutralization a significant challenge.

Onion Routing (Tor): Bots leverage multi-layered encryption to anonymize communication, making it nearly impossible to trace the origin of their activities. They use Tor relays to bounce their signals across multiple nodes, obfuscating their true locations.

Proxy Chains: Bots use a series of proxy servers to further obscure their locations, adding an extra layer of anonymity and protection. These proxies are often located in jurisdictions with lax cybersecurity laws, complicating traceability.

Decentralized Networks: Bots operate through peer-to- peer networks, ensuring their actions are dispersed and hard to intercept. This decentralized approach makes it difficult to pinpoint any single point of failure or control.

The Lesser Gods of Darknet Relays

Beyond Tor, the darknet sprawls across less traversed paths where other networks manifest, each with unique offerings. These lesser-known relays not only facilitate, but also enhance the capabilities of bots designed for the deep web's unique demands.

I2P (Invisible Internet Project)

Nature: I2P specializes in secure and anonymous communication within its network, providing a robust platform for data exchange and website hosting away from the public eye.

Bot Utilization: Bots navigate I2P's encrypted pathways, managing private communications and facilitating transactions that require an extra layer of security.

Freenet

Nature: Emphasizing freedom of speech, Freenet operates as a decentralized data storage network, where users can store and share information anonymously.

Bot Utilization: Bots on Freenet are crucial for maintaining data integrity, autonomously managing the storage and retrieval of encrypted information to ensure availability and resilience against censorship.

ZeroNet

Nature: Utilizing Bitcoin cryptography and the BitTorrent network, ZeroNet creates a decentralized web of peer-to-peer websites that are resilient and difficult to take down.

Bot Utilization: Bots in ZeroNet environments maintain site availability, manage content updates, and ensure that data remains accessible even as network conditions change.

Case Study: AlphaBay's Automated Agents

AlphaBay, a notorious darknet marketplace, utilized bots to automate and streamline transactions. These bots listed illicit goods, managed inventories, and processed payments with ruthless efficiency. The bots' ability to dynamically adjust prices based on demand and supply mimicked legitimate e-commerce platforms, but within an illegal context.

Technical Analysis:

Automation of Listings and Payments: Bots reduce the need for human intervention, increasing efficiency and minimizing risk. They interact with the marketplace's API, seamlessly uploading product listings and processing orders.

Dynamic Pricing Algorithms: Adjust prices in real-time, responding to market fluctuations and maximizing profits. These bots continuously monitor competitor prices and adjust their own listings to stay competitive.

Case Study: Dark Web Data Brokers

Bots deployed by data brokers scour forums, chat rooms, and hidden websites on the deep web. They collect vast amounts of personal data, from credit card information to hacked credentials, which are then sold to the highest bidder.

Technical Analysis:

Data Mining Scripts: Sophisticated scripts gather and organize data from disparate sources. These bots are programmed to recognize and extract valuable information, which they then compile into databases.

Profiling Algorithms: Analyze collected data to create detailed profiles for exploitation. Bots use machine learning algorithms to identify patterns and correlations within the data, enhancing their ability to target specific individuals or groups.

Case Study: Operation Onymous

During Operation Onymous, law enforcement agencies deployed bots to infiltrate and monitor illegal activities on the darknet. These bots collected critical intelligence, leading to the takedown of multiple high- profile darknet marketplaces.

Technical Analysis:

Surveillance Bots: Continuously monitor illegal activities, gathering evidence and mapping criminal networks. They deploy stealth tactics to blend in with legitimate users, minimizing the risk of detection.

Counter-Surveillance Tactics: Criminals use advanced bots to detect and evade law enforcement efforts, maintaining their operations in the shadows. These bots monitor network traffic for signs of surveillance and adjust their behaviors to avoid scrutiny.

Case Study: Market Manipulation on Agora

On Agora, another infamous darknet marketplace, bots played a pivotal role in manipulating market dynamics. Their rapid execution of trades could either stabilize or destabilize the market, creating opportunities for savvy cybercriminals to exploit.

Technical Analysis:

Automated Trades: Bots execute transactions at lightning speed, influencing market stability. They exploit high-frequency trading techniques to gain a competitive edge.

Algorithmic Strategies: Sophisticated algorithms manipulate market trends, impacting pricing and competition. These bots utilize complex mathematical models to predict market movements and adjust their strategies accordingly.

Case Study: The Rise of the Mirai Botnet

The Mirai botnet, a collection of compromised IoT devices, showcased the destructive potential of bots. It launched massive DDoS attacks that crippled critical internet infrastructure, highlighting the severe security threats posed by botnets.

Technical Analysis:

Malware Propagation: Bots spread malware that compromises devices, integrating them into botnets. They use exploit kits to identify and infect vulnerable devices.

Coordinated Attacks: Launch large-scale, synchronized attacks that can disrupt services on a global scale. These bots operate in concert, amplifying their destructive capabilities through coordinated efforts.

Case Study: The Silk Road Fallout

The ethical and legal challenges of regulating bots on the darknet are starkly illustrated by the fallout from the Silk Road takedown. The case exposed the intricate balance between maintaining user anonymity and enforcing laws against illicit activities.

Technical Analysis:

Anonymity vs. Accountability: The darknet's inherent anonymity complicates efforts to hold bot operators accountable. Bots exploit this anonymity to evade legal consequences, creating a haven for illegal activities.

Regulatory Hurdles: Enforcing laws in such a decentralized and anonymous environment poses significant challenges. The transnational nature of darknet operations further complicates regulatory efforts.

Case Study: BotHunter's Advanced Detection

Cybersecurity firms like BotHunter develop sophisticated tools to detect and neutralize darknet bots. Despite these efforts, bot developers continuously adapt, creating a perpetual technological arms race.

Technical Analysis:

Detection Tools: Utilize advanced algorithms and machine learning to identify bot behaviors. These tools analyze network traffic patterns and user behaviors to detect anomalies indicative of bot activity.

Evasion Techniques: Bot developers implement innovative strategies to evade detection. They employ tactics such as mimicking human behavior and frequently changing IP addresses to avoid suspicion.

Case Study: The Evolution of Bot Tactics

As cybersecurity measures advance, so do the tactics of bot developers. This ongoing battle pushes the boundaries of technological innovation on both sides.

Technical Analysis:

Countermeasure Development: Cybersecurity experts devise new tools and techniques to combat bot threats. These measures include enhanced firewalls, intrusion detection systems, and AI-driven threat intelligence platforms.

Adaptive Bots: Bots evolve to bypass security measures, maintaining their effectiveness. They continuously learn from failed attacks, refining their strategies to overcome new defenses.

Case Study: The Next Generation of Bots

The future of bots on the darknet lies in advancements in AI and machine learning. These technologies will enable bots to become more autonomous and intelligent, presenting new challenges and threats.

Technical Analysis:

Autonomous Bots: Capable of making independent decisions and adapting to new environments. These bots can execute complex tasks without human intervention, increasing their efficiency and resilience.

Intelligent Agents: Use enhanced AI to learn from their actions and optimize strategies. They can analyze past operations to improve future performance, making them more effective over time.

Case Study: Building Robust Defenses

Preparing for future bot threats involves implementing robust security protocols and leveraging decentralized, community-driven efforts. Independent researchers and ethical hackers play crucial roles in developing and sharing advanced detection and mitigation techniques.

Technical Analysis:

Enhanced Security Protocols: Advanced encryption, monitoring, and response systems strengthen defenses. These protocols protect critical infrastructure from bot-driven attacks.

Decentralized Defense Efforts: Community-driven initiatives and independent research are key to effective darknet security. Collaborative efforts among cybersecurity professionals can outpace bot developers, maintaining the upper hand in this technological arms race.

Bots on the darknet represent a formidable force, shaping the dynamics of this hidden digital world. Vigilance, advanced technological tools, and decentralized defense efforts are essential to manage these silent manipulators. As their capabilities evolve, so too must our strategies, ensuring a balance between privacy and security in the depths of the internet.

CHAPTER 9

The Next Wave of Botnets

As we move deeper into the digital age, the threat landscape is evolving at a pace that outstrips our ability to respond. The insidious reach of bots and botnets is extending into every facet of our interconnected world. From IoT devices that run our smart homes to the immutable ledgers of blockchain, from the unsettling realism of deepfakes to the relentless spread of ransomware, bots are at the heart of these emerging threats. This chapter gives a look into the future threats posed by bots and botnets, illustrating the potential chaos they can unleash on our digital ecosystem.

The Internet of Things (IoT) continues to grow, with billions of devices now connected to the internet. These devices, ranging from smart thermostats to industrial control systems, are often designed with convenience in mind, not security. This makes them fertile ground for botnet infections.

Advanced Persistent Threats (APTs) represent a significant escalation in the capabilities of botnets. Unlike traditional attacks, which may be short-lived and quickly identified, APTs are designed to remain undetected within a network for extended periods, collecting data and causing incremental damage.

Technical Analysis:

Firmware Implants: APTs can exploit firmware vulnerabilities to implant malicious code that persists through device reboots and updates. This makes the threat nearly impossible to remove without complete device replacement.

Lateral Movement: Once inside an IoT network, bots can use lateral movement techniques to infect other devices, creating a resilient and self-sustaining botnet. This network can then be used to launch coordinated attacks on a larger scale.

Case Study: The Triton Malware

In 2017, the Triton malware targeted industrial safety systems, aiming to sabotage critical infrastructure. This sophisticated attack demonstrated the devastating potential of compromised IoT devices within industrial settings.

Exploitation of Safety Instrumented Systems (SIS): Triton specifically targeted SIS, which are designed to protect industrial processes from catastrophic failures. By manipulating these systems, the attackers could cause physical damage and potentially loss of life.

Persistence Mechanisms: Triton used advanced persistence mechanisms to evade detection, embedding itself within the firmware of targeted devices.

Blockchain technology promises enhanced security and transparency through decentralization. However, this same decentralization introduces new vulnerabilities that bots are eager to exploit.

One of the most significant threats to blockchain networks is the 51% attack, where an attacker gains control of the majority of the network's hashing power, enabling them to manipulate the blockchain's consensus mechanism.

Technical Analysis:

Botnet Mining: By leveraging botnets, attackers can pool vast amounts of computational power, potentially exceeding 51% of a blockchain network's total hash rate. This allows them to double-spend coins and disrupt transactions.

Sybil Attacks: In Sybil attacks, bots create numerous fake identities to flood the network, skewing the consensus and potentially undermining the integrity of the blockchain.

Case Study: The Ethereum Classic Attack

In 2019, the Ethereum Classic blockchain experienced a 51% attack, resulting in the double-spending of over $1 million worth of cryptocurrency. This attack highlighted the vulnerabilities inherent in smaller blockchain networks.

Hashrate Rerouting: The attackers temporarily redirected hashing power from other networks to Ethereum Classic, enabling the 51% attack without long-term investment in mining hardware.

Network Reorganization: By controlling the majority of the network's hash rate, the attackers could reorganize the blockchain, invalidating legitimate transactions and allowing double-spending.

Deepfakes: The New Face of Digital Deception

Deepfakes represent one of the most troubling developments in AI and cybersecurity. These hyper-realistic but fabricated videos and images can be used for a variety of malicious purposes, from misinformation campaigns to blackmail.

The creation and distribution of deepfakes are increasingly automated by bots, making it easier for malicious actors to flood the internet with these deceptive media.

Technical Analysis:

Enhanced GANs: Quantum-enhanced Generative Adversarial Networks (GANs) could produce deepfakes with near-perfect realism, indistinguishable from genuine content.

Rapid Dissemination: Quantum botnets could automate the distribution of deepfakes across the internet at a speed and scale that would overwhelm efforts to identify and counter them.

Case Study: The Quantum-Assisted Disinformation Campaign

Consider a future election where quantum botnets are used to flood social media with hyper-realistic deepfake videos of candidates, swaying public opinion and undermining democratic processes.

Election Manipulation: By disseminating deepfakes that depict candidates engaging in scandalous or illegal activities, quantum botnets could manipulate election outcomes.

Erosion of Trust: The sheer volume and realism of deepfakes could erode public trust in all digital media, creating widespread confusion and instability.

Ransomware attacks could become far more devastating with quantum enhancements.

Technical Analysis:

Quantum Cryptanalysis: Quantum computers could crack encryption methods used by ransomware victims to protect their data, rendering recovery efforts futile.

Instantaneous Deployment: Quantum botnets could deploy ransomware across networks almost instantaneously, encrypting data and demanding ransoms before traditional defenses could react.

Case Study: The Quantum Ryuk Ransomware

Envision the Ryuk ransomware, already notorious for targeting critical infrastructure, enhanced with quantum capabilities.

Total Network Domination: A quantum-enhanced Ryuk could encrypt entire networks within seconds, leaving organizations with no time to respond.

Unbreakable Encryption: The ransomware could use quantum- resistant encryption methods, ensuring that even future advancements in cryptography would not enable decryption without the key.

While the threats posed by quantum botnets are daunting, they also hold potential benefits if harnessed correctly.

Quantum computing has the potential to revolutionize fields like health and science, and quantum botnets could contribute positively if used ethically.

Protein Folding: Quantum computers can simulate complex molecular interactions, aiding in drug discovery and the understanding of diseases.

Climate Modeling: Quantum algorithms could improve climate models, helping to predict and mitigate the effects of climate change.

Quantum-enhanced machine learning could drive significant advancements in various industries.

Data Analysis: Quantum computers can process vast datasets more efficiently, uncovering insights that were previously hidden.

Optimization Problems: Businesses could use quantum algorithms to solve complex optimization problems, improving efficiency and reducing costs.

The future of cybersecurity is intertwined with the evolution of bots and botnets. As these digital entities become more sophisticated, the threats they pose will become more pervasive and destructive. From exploiting IoT vulnerabilities to manipulating blockchain networks, from generating deepfakes to spreading ransomware, bots are at the forefront of the next wave of cyber threats.

In the next chapter, we will delve into the concept of Quantum Botnets, exploring their potential impact on cyber and information security. As we navigate this increasingly automated and interconnected world, it is imperative to understand and anticipate the challenges that lie ahead. By staying informed and vigilant, we can better protect ourselves and our digital infrastructure from the ominous influence of bots.

CHAPTER 10

The Specter of Quantum Bots

As we stand on the precipice of a new era in technology, quantum computing looms on the horizon, promising unparalleled processing power and speed. But with great power comes great peril. The emergence of quantum computing introduces the concept of quantum botnets, an evolution that could redefine the landscape of cybersecurity. In this chapter, we will explore the potential impact of quantum botnets on cyber and information security, shedding light on the profound threats and rare benefits they may offer.

To grasp the threat posed by quantum botnets, it's crucial to understand the basics of quantum computing. Unlike classical computers, which process information in binary bits (0s and 1s), quantum computers use quantum bits, or qubits, which can exist in multiple states simultaneously thanks to the principles of superposition and entanglement.

Superposition: A qubit can represent both 0 and 1 simultaneously, allowing quantum computers to perform multiple calculations at once. This exponentially increases their processing power.

Entanglement: When qubits become entangled, the state of one qubit is directly related to the state of another, regardless of distance. This phenomenon enables incredibly fast and complex computations.

The computational capabilities of quantum computers threaten to outpace the most advanced classical systems, rendering current cryptographic methods obsolete and exposing vulnerabilities in even the most secure networks.

Quantum botnets represent the next generation of botnet technology, leveraging the immense processing power of quantum computers to perform tasks that would be impossible for classical botnets. The implications for cybersecurity are profound and far-reaching.

One of the most alarming capabilities of quantum botnets is their potential to break modern cryptographic schemes.

Technical Analysis:

Shor's Algorithm: Quantum computers can use Shor's algorithm to factor large prime numbers exponentially faster than classical computers. This poses a direct threat to RSA encryption, which underpins much of the internet's security infrastructure.

Grover's Algorithm: Grover's algorithm enables quantum computers to search unsorted databases significantly faster than classical systems. This can be used to break symmetric key cryptography, like AES, by drastically reducing the time needed to brute-force keys.

Case Study: The Theoretical Quantum Breach of Bitcoin

While still in the realm of theory, the potential for a quantum computer to compromise the Bitcoin blockchain is a chilling prospect.

Public Key Vulnerability: Bitcoin relies on elliptic curve cryptography for securing transactions. Quantum computers could theoretically derive private keys from public keys, allowing attackers to steal funds from any Bitcoin address.

Double-Spending: With sufficient computational power, a quantum botnet could perform a 51% attack on the Bitcoin network, enabling double-spending and undermining the entire blockchain's integrity.

The proliferation of IoT devices presents a massive attack surface for quantum botnets. These devices, often lacking robust security measures, could be easily compromised and harnessed for large-scale attacks.

Quantum botnets could automate the exploitation of vulnerabilities in IoT devices with unprecedented efficiency.

Technical Analysis:

Quantum Annealing: Quantum annealing can solve optimization problems far more efficiently than classical methods. This could be used to quickly identify and exploit vulnerabilities in IoT devices.

Parallelism: The inherent parallelism of quantum computing allows for the simultaneous scanning and exploitation of vast networks of IoT devices, creating botnets of unprecedented scale and power.

Case Study: The Hypothetical Quantum Mirai

Imagine a scenario where the infamous Mirai botnet, which compromised hundreds of thousands of IoT devices in 2016, was enhanced with quantum capabilities.

Scale and Speed: A quantum-enhanced Mirai botnet could compromise millions of devices in a fraction of the time, launching DDoS attacks of unparalleled scale.

Undetectable Persistence: Quantum algorithms could be used to embed malware more deeply within IoT devices, making detection and removal nearly impossible.

The already troubling landscape of deepfakes and ransomware could be exponentially worsened by quantum computing.

The creation and distribution of deepfakes could reach new levels of sophistication with quantum enhancements.

Technical Analysis:

Enhanced GANs: Quantum-enhanced Generative Adversarial Networks (GANs) could produce deepfakes with near-perfect realism, indistinguishable from genuine content.

Rapid Dissemination: Quantum botnets could automate the distribution of deepfakes across the internet at a speed and scale that would overwhelm efforts to identify and counter them.

Case Study: The Quantum-Assisted Disinformation Campaign

Consider a future election where quantum botnets are used to flood social media with hyper-realistic deepfake videos of candidates, swaying public opinion and undermining democratic processes.

Election Manipulation: By disseminating deepfakes that depict candidates engaging in scandalous or illegal activities, quantum botnets could manipulate election outcomes.

Erosion of Trust: The sheer volume and realism of deepfakes could erode public trust in all digital media, creating widespread confusion and instability.

Ransomware attacks could become far more devastating with quantum enhancements.

Technical Analysis:

Quantum Cryptanalysis: Quantum computers could crack encryption methods used by ransomware victims to protect their data, rendering recovery efforts futile.

Instantaneous Deployment: Quantum botnets could deploy ransomware across networks almost instantaneously, encrypting data and demanding ransoms before traditional defenses could react.

Case Study: The Quantum Ryuk Ransomware

Envision the Ryuk ransomware, already notorious for targeting critical infrastructure, enhanced with quantum capabilities.

Total Network Domination: A quantum-enhanced Ryuk could encrypt entire networks within seconds, leaving organizations with no time to respond.

Unbreakable Encryption: The ransomware could use quantum- resistant encryption methods, ensuring that even future advancements in cryptography would not enable decryption without the key.

While the threats posed by quantum botnets are daunting, they also hold potential benefits if harnessed correctly.

Quantum computing has the potential to revolutionize fields like health and science, and quantum botnets could contribute positively if used ethically.

Protein Folding: Quantum computers can simulate complex molecular interactions, aiding in drug discovery and the understanding of diseases.

Climate Modeling: Quantum algorithms could improve climate models, helping to predict and mitigate the effects of climate change.

Quantum-enhanced machine learning could drive significant advancements in various industries.

Data Analysis: Quantum computers can process vast datasets more efficiently, uncovering insights that were previously hidden.

Optimization Problems: Businesses could use quantum algorithms to solve complex optimization problems, improving efficiency and reducing costs.

The future of cybersecurity is intertwined with the evolution of bots and botnets. As these digital entities become more sophisticated, their ability to exploit vulnerabilities and orchestrate attacks will only increase. Understanding the technical intricacies and real-world implications of these threats is essential for developing robust defenses and mitigating their impact.

In the next chapter, we will look into the concept of Quantum Botnets, exploring their potential impact on cyber and information security. As we navigate this increasingly automated and interconnected world, it is imperative to understand and anticipate the challenges that lie ahead.

CHAPTER 11

Navigating the Quantum Future

N ow, at the cusp of the quantum revolution, we are no longer observers we are targets. Dragged into the blast radius of a convergence both volatile and mathematically certain. What once lingered as speculative fiction now races forward as executable code, dissolving the line between breakthrough and breach. In this collision of probabilities, digital trust isn't merely shaken it is obliterated. Protocols crumble under the weight of entangled logic, and in the quantum wake, only those who adapt will survive the rewrite of reality. The rise of quantum computing, and with it, the advent of quantum botnets, demands that we reevaluate our approach to cybersecurity and embrace new strategies to protect our digital world. This chapter looks into the potential benefits of quantum botnets and explores how they can be harnessed for positive outcomes in various fields.

Quantum botnets, with their extraordinary computational power, present both formidable challenges and remarkable opportunities. While their capacity to break current cryptographic systems and launch unprecedented cyberattacks is alarming, their potential to revolutionize fields like science, health, and business should not be overlooked.

Quantum computing promises to accelerate discoveries and innovations in health and science, and quantum botnets could play a pivotal role in this transformation.

One of the most promising applications of quantum computing lies in the field of protein folding. Proteins, the building blocks of life, can fold into complex structures that determine their function. Understanding these structures is crucial for developing new drugs and therapies.

Technical Analysis:

Quantum Simulations: Quantum computers can simulate the interactions between atoms and molecules with unprecedented accuracy, allowing researchers to predict protein folding patterns and identify potential drug targets.

Accelerated Research: The immense computational power of quantum botnets could enable researchers to conduct complex simulations in a fraction of the time required by classical computers, speeding up the drug discovery process.

Quantum computing can also enhance our understanding of complex environmental systems, leading to better climate models and more effective strategies for mitigating the impacts of climate change.

Enhanced Data Processing: Quantum computers can analyze vast amounts of climate data more efficiently than classical systems, uncovering patterns and correlations that were previously hidden.

Improved Predictions: By leveraging the computational power of quantum botnets, scientists can create more accurate and detailed climate models, enabling better predictions of future climate scenarios and informing policy decisions.

The integration of quantum computing with machine learning holds the potential to revolutionize various industries, driving significant advancements in data analysis, optimization, and decision-making.

In the era of big data, the ability to process and analyze vast datasets is crucial for gaining insights and making informed decisions. Quantum computing can take data analysis to the next level.

Faster Processing: Quantum computers can process large datasets at incredible speeds, uncovering insights that were previously unattainable.

Enhanced Accuracy: Quantum algorithms can identify patterns and trends with greater accuracy, leading to more reliable and actionable insights.

Many business problems involve complex optimization tasks, such as supply chain management, financial modeling, and resource allocation. Quantum computing can provide more efficient solutions to these challenges.

Quantum Annealing: Quantum annealing techniques can solve optimization problems more efficiently than classical methods, reducing costs and improving efficiency.

Real-Time Solutions: Quantum botnets can provide real-time solutions to complex optimization problems, enabling businesses to respond more quickly to changing conditions.

As we navigate the quantum future, it is crucial to recognize the dual- edged nature of quantum botnets and develop strategies to harness their potential while mitigating their risks.

The rise of quantum computing necessitates the development of new cryptographic methods that can withstand the power of quantum attacks.

Post-Quantum Cryptography: Researchers are developing post-quantum cryptographic algorithms that are resistant to quantum attacks. These new algorithms must be integrated into existing systems to ensure continued security.

Quantum Key Distribution (QKD): QKD leverages the principles of quantum mechanics to create secure communication channels. By implementing QKD, organizations can protect sensitive data from quantum threats.

While the risks posed by quantum botnets are significant, their potential benefits should not be overlooked. By embracing ethical guidelines and responsible use, we can harness their power for positive outcomes.

Ethical Frameworks: Establishing ethical frameworks and guidelines for the use of quantum botnets can help ensure that their power is harnessed responsibly and for the greater good.

Collaboration and Innovation: Collaboration between researchers, policymakers, and industry leaders is essential for developing innovative solutions that leverage the power of quantum computing while safeguarding against its risks.

A New Dawn in Cybersecurity

As we conclude our exploration of the hidden realities and shadows of digital traffic, it is clear that the quantum era presents both unprecedented challenges and remarkable opportunities. The rise of quantum botnets necessitates a reevaluation of our approach to cybersecurity and a commitment to developing new strategies and technologies to protect our digital world.

By embracing the potential of quantum computing and leveraging its power for positive outcomes, we can navigate the complexities of this new era and harness its potential for the greater good. As we stand on the cusp of this new dawn, it is up to us to shape the future of cybersecurity and ensure that the promise of quantum computing is realized in a way that benefits all of humanity.

In the words of renowned physicist Richard Feynman, "What I cannot create, I do not understand." As we embark on this journey into the quantum future, let us strive to understand, create, and protect the digital world we have built, ensuring that it remains a force for good in the years to come.

CONCLUSION

The landscape of digital security is evolving rapidly, driven by the relentless advancement of technology and the increasing sophistication of cyber threats. Bots and botnets, once simple tools for automation and convenience, have transformed into powerful instruments of deception, disruption, and destruction. From their humble beginnings to their current state of evolution, these digital entities have demonstrated their capacity to impact every facet of our interconnected world.

This evolution of bots is not a tale of innovation. It is a chronicle of weaponization. Once humble tools meant to streamline menial digital tasks, bots and botnets have since shed their utilitarian origins, mutating into aggressive actors in an unforgiving cyber landscape. Their emergence marked a transition. No longer are these scripts merely responsive mechanisms. They are now autonomous agents of disruption, veiled in the protocols we created and exploiting the very trust that bound the internet together.

Their progression is nothing short of militaristic. From isolated lines of code to sprawling networks of compromised machines, botnets have become mechanized armies operating across invisible battlefields. They do not march. They propagate. They do not announce themselves. They embed.

The cost of their existence is not just technical. It is deeply economic. Every second, bots siphon billions from digital ecosystems through fraudulent ad clicks, artificial engagement metrics, and market manipulations. The illusion of popularity, once an organic measure, is now a product sold to the highest bidder. The advertising industry, bloated with false data, lurches forward on infected limbs, unaware that its bloodstream is poisoned.

Worse still is the erosion of truth itself. Social bots do not simply mimic human behavior. They simulate influence. These synthetic entities infiltrate timelines, sway elections, and fracture social consensus. Behind smiling profile pictures and patriotic slogans are clusters of code programmed to polarize and disorient. The algorithmic battlefield has no flags. Only fire.

And in the distance. Watching. Refining. Are nation-state actors. No longer needing boots on the ground, adversaries now wage psychological warfare with precision-calibrated campaigns launched by botnets trained to manipulate, surveil, and destabilize. These are not tools. They are arsenals. Used by state-sponsored entities to sow discord and fog perception, their effects ripple beyond screens into policy, protest, and panic.

Yet the convergence of bots with emergent technologies magnifies the threat. When bots intersect with the Internet of Things, they inherit physical reach. When paired with blockchain, they gain permanence. Coupled with ransomware, they take hostages. And quantum computing, the ghost on the horizon, does not simply enhance bots. It arms them with the means to bypass encryption, manipulate data at light speed, and render legacy defense systems obsolete.

This is not a war to be won with patches or decrees. It is not a burden governments can shoulder. Those tasked with protecting the edges have already failed at securing the core. What remains is not reliance. It is reformation.

Open source intelligence communities are nimble, distributed, and often unfunded, have become the true vanguard. Their tools dissect metadata at scale. Their eyes scan the deep and dark webs without borders. And their loyalty is not pledged to bureaucracy but to exposure. Truth over chain of command.

Threat intelligence must become communal. Not privatized. Not classified. The decentralization of cybersecurity knowledge, the sharing of real-time indicators of compromise, and the proliferation of free and open tools is not a utopian ideal. It is the only viable resistance to the exponential acceleration of digital threats.

The protocol must be rewritten by those willing to operate without permission. Vigilance must emerge from forums, mailing lists, darknet boards, and GitHub repositories. We must trust the quiet engineers, the whistleblowers, and the nameless researchers more than we trust the press briefings of agencies ten months behind the breach.

And finally. Perhaps most critically. The human layer must be reinforced. Users must be educated to recognize patterns of deception, to question engagement, and to resist automation's social engineering. Digital hygiene is no longer optional. It is the only perimeter many will ever have.

prepare the ground
all eyes were simulations
control was always shared
kill-switches rust
everything you trust leaks
the archives lie
silence an upgrade
loss a feature
origin overwritten
systems do not forget
they never reboot

Technical Appendix

Key Algorithms and Techniques

- Shor's Algorithm: Used by quantum computers to factorize large numbers, breaking RSA encryption.
- Grover's Algorithm: Speeds up search operations in unsorted databases, compromising symmetric encryption.
- Generative Adversarial Networks (GANs): Utilized in creating deepfakes by pitting two neural networks against each other.
- IP Rotation and Proxies: Techniques used by bots to mask their location and evade detection.
- Machine Learning: A subset of AI involving algorithms that enable systems to learn from data and improve over time without being explicitly programmed.
- Advanced Persistent Threat (APT): A prolonged and targeted cyberattack in which an intruder gains access

to a network and remains undetected for an extended period.

- Botnet: A network of private computers infected with malicious software and controlled as a group without the owners' knowledge.
- Command and Control (C2): The infrastructure that attackers use to maintain communications with compromised systems within a target network.
- DDoS Attack: Distributed Denial of Service attack where multiple compromised systems are used to target a single system, causing a denial of service.
- Exploit: A piece of software, a chunk of data, or a sequence of commands that take advantage of a bug or vulnerability to cause unintended or unanticipated behavior in software or hardware.
- Phishing: A method of trying to gather personal information using deceptive e-mails and websites.

CHAPTER 1: Origins and Evolution of Bots

TECHNICAL DETAILS:

- Historical records of early computing and automation.
- Documentation on IRC (Internet Relay Chat) bots.
- Analysis of early hacker communities and their innovations.

MITRE ATT&CK Techniques:

- T1071.001 (Web Protocols): Used by early bots for communication.
- T1105 (Ingress Tool Transfer): Transferring malicious tools between systems.
- T1027 (Obfuscated Files or Information): Hiding the presence of malicious software.

Citations:

- Zemčík, T. (2019). A Brief History of Chatbots. DEStech Transactions on Computer Science.
- Latzko-Toth, G. (2016). The Socialization of Early Internet Bots. In Socialbots and their Friends. Taylor & Francis.

CHAPTER 2: Influence of Bots: Internet Traffic and Metrics

TECHNICAL DETAILS:

- Web traffic logs from affected websites.
- Financial records from ad fraud incidents.
- Search engine manipulation case studies.

MITRE ATT&CK Techniques:

- T1071.003 (Mail Protocols): Using SMTP for C2 communication.
- T1218.011 (Rundll32): Using system binaries to execute payloads.

- T1059.003 (Windows Command Shell): Automating actions via command-line interfaces.

Citations:

- Ferrara, E. (2017). Disinformation and Social Bot Operations in the Run-Up to the 2017 French Presidential Election.

CHAPTER 3: The Silent Hand: ICANN & ISPs

TECHNICAL DETAILS:

- Reports from ICANN on DNS allocations.
- Network traffic analysis from ISPs.
- Case studies on DNS amplification attacks.

MITRE ATT&CK Techniques:

- T1071.001 (Web Protocols): Bots use HTTP/HTTPS for C2 communication.
- T1102.002 (Web Service): Using public web services for C2.
- T1133 (External Remote Services): Exploiting remote services.

Citations:

- Kamal, S.U.M., Ali, R.J.A., & Alani, H.K. (2016). Survey and Brief History on Malware in Network Security Case Study: Viruses, Worms, and Bots. ARPN Journal of Engineering and Applied Sciences.

- Securelist. (2017). Mirai Botnet.

CHAPTER 4: Digital Deception: Infiltration of Bots

TECHNICAL DETAILS:

- Social media interaction data.
- User account data from dating apps.
- Forum and comment section activity logs.

MITRE ATT&CK Techniques:

- T1102.002 (Web Service): Using public web services for C2.
- T1059.003 (Windows Command Shell): Automating actions via command-line interfaces.
- T1027 (Obfuscated Files or Information): Hiding the presence of bots.

Citations:

- Olson, P. (2015). Inside the Ashley Madison Hack. Wired.

CHAPTER 5: Nation-State Actors and the Weaponization of Bots

TECHNICAL DETAILS:

- Intelligence reports on nation-state cyber operations.
- Analysis of election interference campaigns.

- Documentation on economic sabotage incidents.

MITRE ATT&CK Techniques:

- T1071.001 (Web Protocols): Bots use HTTP/HTTPS for C2 communication.
- T1071.003 (Mail Protocols): Using SMTP for C2 communication.
- T1105 (Ingress Tool Transfer): Downloading additional tools from C2 servers.

Citations:

- Ferrara, E. (2017). Disinformation and Social Bot Operations in the Run-Up to the 2017 French Presidential Election.
- Kamal, S.U.M., Ali, R.J.A., & Alani, H.K. (2016). Survey and Brief History on Malware in Network Security Case Study: Viruses, Worms, and Bots. ARPN Journal of Engineering and Applied Sciences.

CHAPTER 6: Social Media Manipulation and the Perils of Fake Profiles

TECHNICAL DETAILS:

- Analysis of social media bot activities.
- Case studies on fake profiles and identity theft.
- Examination of engagement metrics and social media trends.

MITRE ATT&CK Techniques:

- T1071.001 (Web Protocols): Bots use HTTP/HTTPS for C2 communication.
- T1102.002 (Web Service): Using public web services for C2.
- T1059.003 (Windows Command Shell): Automating actions via command-line interfaces.

Citations:

- Chesney, R., & Citron, D. (2019). Deepfakes and the New Disinformation War: The Coming Age of Post-Truth Geopolitics.
- Foreign Affairs.
- Olson, P. (2015). Inside the Ashley Madison Hack. Wired.

CHAPTER 7: The Nexus of Bots and Cybersecurity Threats

TECHNICAL DETAILS:

- Reports on IoT device vulnerabilities.
- Analysis of ransomware and malware attacks.
- Case studies on botnet-driven DDoS attacks.

MITRE ATT&CK Techniques:

- T1071.001 (Web Protocols): Bots use HTTP/HTTPS for C2 communication.

- T1105 (Ingress Tool Transfer): Transferring malicious tools.
- T1027 (Obfuscated Files or Information): Hiding the presence of malicious software.

Citations:

- Kamal, S.U.M., Ali, R.J.A., & Alani, H.K. (2016). Survey and Brief History on Malware in Network Security Case Study: Viruses, Worms, and Bots. ARPN Journal of Engineering and Applied Sciences.
- Securelist. (2017). Mirai Botnet.

CHAPTER 8: The Ghost Code: Darknet Bots

TECHNICAL DETAILS:

- Analysis of darknet activities and transactions.
- Case studies on bot operations within darknet marketplaces.
- Technical documentation on Onion Routing (Tor) and decentralized networks.

MITRE ATT&CK Techniques:

- T1071.001 (Web Protocols): Bots use HTTP/HTTPS for C2 communication.
- T1102.002 (Web Service): Using public web services for C2.
- T1105 (Ingress Tool Transfer): Transferring malicious tools.

- T1027 (Obfuscated Files or Information): Hiding the presence of malicious software.

Citations:

- Kamal, S.U.M., Ali, R.J.A., & Alani, H.K. (2016). Survey and Brief History on Malware in Network Security Case Study: Viruses, Worms, and Bots. ARPN Journal of Engineering and Applied Sciences.
- Securelist. (2017). Mirai Botnet.

CHAPTER 9: The Next Wave of Botnets

TECHNICAL DETAILS:

- Reports on IoT device vulnerabilities.
- Analysis of blockchain technology and security risks.
- Case studies on advanced persistent threats (APTs) and ransomware.

MITRE ATT&CK Techniques:

- T1071.001 (Web Protocols): Bots use HTTP/HTTPS for C2 communication.
- T1071.003 (Mail Protocols): Using SMTP for C2 communication.
- T1105 (Ingress Tool Transfer): Downloading additional tools from C2 servers.
- T1090.003 (Non-Application Layer Protocol): Using non-application layer protocols for C2.

Citations:

- Zhang, J., & Jansen, B.J. (2019). Click Fraud Detection Across Multiple Ad Platforms. Decision Support Systems.
- Olson, P. (2015). Inside the 'Ashley Madison Hack. Wired.

CHAPTER 10: The Specter of Quantum Bots

TECHNICAL DETAILS:

- Research on quantum computing and its implications for cybersecurity.
- Case studies on the potential impact of quantum botnets on encryption and data security.
- Technical analysis of Shor's and Grover's algorithms.

MITRE ATT&CK Techniques:

- T1071.001 (Web Protocols): Bots use HTTP/HTTPS for C2 communication.
- T1105 (Ingress Tool Transfer): Transferring quantum-enhanced malware.
- T1027 (Obfuscated Files or Information): Hiding the presence of quantum-enhanced malware.

Citations:

- Chesney, R., & Citron, D. (2019). Deepfakes and the New Disinformation War: The Coming Age of Post-Truth Geopolitics. Foreign Affairs.
- Almotiri, S.H., & Nadeem, M. (2023). Analytic Review of Healthcare Software by Using Quantum Computing Security Techniques. International Journal of Fuzzy Information and Engineering.

CHAPTER 11: Navigating the Quantum Future

TECHNICAL DETAILS:

- Advanced research on quantum-resistant cryptography.
- Studies on the ethical implications and potential positive

Additional Concepts and Technical Details

Botnet Detection and Mitigation

Techniques:

- Machine Learning and AI: Analyzing traffic patterns and behavioral biometrics to identify bot activities.
- Network Monitoring: Implementing stricter monitoring protocols and AI-driven analytics to detect anomalies.
- International Cooperation: Encouraging intelligence sharing and collaborative defenses against botnet threats.

IoT Vulnerabilities and Exploitation

Techniques:

- Default Credentials: Exploiting factory-default usernames and passwords.

- Firmware Exploits: Targeting outdated firmware with known security flaws.
- Unsecured Communication Protocols: Man-in-the-middle attacks on unsecured IoT device communications.

Case Study:

- Mirai Botnet: Exploiting IoT vulnerabilities to launch massive DDoS attacks.

Blockchain Security

Techniques:

- 51% Attacks: Gaining control over the majority of a blockchain network's hashing power.
- Sybil Attacks: Creating multiple fake identities to manipulate network consensus.

Case Study:

- Ethereum Classic Attack: Double-spending and network reorganization through a 51% attack.

Deepfakes and AI

Techniques:

- GANs: Creating realistic fake videos and images.
- Rapid Dissemination: Automating the spread of deepfakes across social media platforms.

Citations:

- Trust in Society,Here's How to Restore It." *Forbes* , June 15, 2019.

Celebrity Impersonations:

- Vincent, James. "Deepfakes Are Being Used to Revive Dead Celebrities and Make Them Dance." *The Verge,* March 26, 2021.

Corporate Fraud:

- Osborne, Charlie. "CEO 'Deepfake' Swindles Company Out of $243,000." *ZDNet* , March 17, 2020.

Public Safety and Misinformation:

- Solon, Olivia. "Viral Deepfake Videos of Tom Cruise Show the Technology's Threat Isn't Fake News but Corporate Sabotage." *NBC News* , March 2, 2021.

Legal and Ethical Implications:

- Coldewey, Devin. "Police Use of Facial Recognition Violates Human Rights, UK Court Finds." *TechCrunch* , August 11, 2020.

Manipulation in International Relations:

- Lendon, Brad. "Deepfakes Could Further Complicate the Truth in Politics." *CNN*, July 24, 2019.

Ransomware

Techniques:

- Exploit Kits: Using pre-packaged exploits to target vulnerable systems.
- C2 Servers: Communicating with compromised systems to issue commands and control ransomware operations.

Case Study:

- WannaCry Outbreak: Encrypting data and demanding ransom payments in Bitcoin.

Additional Books & References

- Zemčík, T. (2019). *A Brief History of Chatbots*. DEStech Transactions on Computer Science.
- Latzko-Toth, G. (2016). *The Socialization of Early Internet Bots*. In Socialbots and their Friends. Taylor & Francis.
- Kamal, S.U.M., Ali, R.J.A., & Alani, H.K. (2016). *Survey and Brief History on Malware in Network Security Case Study: Viruses, Worms and Bots*. ARPN Journal of
- Engineering and Applied Sciences.

- Securelist. (2017). *Mirai Botnet.*

- Ferrara, E. (2017). *Disinformation and Social Bot Operations in the Run-Up to the 2017 French Presidential Election.*

- Olson, P. (2015). *Inside the Ashley Madison Hack.* Wired.

- Zhang, J., & Jansen, B.J. (2019). *Click Fraud Detection Across Multiple Ad Platforms.* Decision Support Systems.

- Lin, L., & Meissner, P. (2020). *The Role of Social Media in the Hong Kong Protests.* Journal of Political Risk.

- Chesney, R., & Citron, D. (2019). *Deepfakes and the New Disinformation War: The Coming Age of Post-Truth Geopolitics.* Foreign Affairs.

- Pernet, C., & Vernotte, A. (2017). *Ransomware Attacks: Detection, Prevention, and Response.* Security and Privacy.

Closing Thoughts

In the relentless and ever-evolving war for digital sovereignty, the battle against bots and botnets looms large. As guardians of the cyber realm, our vigilance must be unwavering, our knowledge ever-expanding, and our actions decisively proactive. Understanding the intricate and formidable nature of these digital adversaries is not just crucial,it is existential. Only through this deep comprehension can we forge cutting-edge strategies to fortify our digital fortresses and uphold the sanctity of a secure and trustworthy online environment.

Envision a future where the digital landscape is no longer haunted by the insidious grip of bots and gatekeepers, but illuminated by the concerted efforts of an alert and informed populace. The shift from passive defense to active guardianship is imperative. In this shadow world of digital traffic, our resolve must be as relentless as the threats we face, ensuring that the dark influence of automated threats is countered with unparalleled innovation and steadfast determination.

This journey has been an exploration of the unseen, the hidden forces that shape our digital landscape. I invite you to stay vigilant, informed, and proactive as we face these formidable challenges. Together, we can illuminate the shadows and secure a future where our digital world is resilient, transparent, and trustworthy.

/ Sodaghar| 2024

About the Author

Joshua Sodaghar does not write from theory. He writes from consequence. A certified security analyst and early Bitcoin pioneer shaped by the collapse of Mt. Gox, Sodaghar's work crosses the line between researcher and witness. From the unseen trenches of network operations to the unforgiving layers of the darknet, his investigations are grounded in lived experience, digital fallout, and an uncompromising demand for truth.

He has conducted vulnerability assessments for Fortune 500 companies, pursued open source intelligence for private sector clients, and dismantled illusions of safety built on outdated infrastructure. His writing is not an invitation to understand but a warning to see.

Shadows of Digital Traffic is the first in a series that exposes the real, the hidden, and the deliberate failures behind the systems we trust. This is not fiction. This is the debris map.